An Easy Guide To Healing

by

Ash Kotecha

Fresh Wind Publications

Copyright © 2009 by Ash Kotecha

ISBN: 978-0-9561861-0-2

Published by
Fresh Wind Publications
17, Edzell Crescent
Westcroft
Milton Keynes
MK4 4EU

Table of Contents

Foreword

Healing is a vast subject and this guide is by no means comprehensive but I have tried to make it easy for anyone to learn some of the lessons I've learnt. There was a time I wished to be in the healing ministry but I was too scared of failing. Now it's been a number of years and we've seen the blind see, deaf ears open, cripples walking, cancers healed and almost every other ailment healed from diabetes to arthritis, all kinds of pain, ME, MS—you name it, we've seen God do hundreds of miracles.

If God can do it for me, He can do it for anyone who will dare to believe and put into practice the principles I've outlined in this guide. The world is full of sceptics, but one thing is for sure, Jesus still heals people today. He has not changed and as the scripture says, He is the same yesterday, today and forever. There are so many sick and hurting people and my prayer is that this guide will help you not only receive your healing but also help others receive theirs too.

God bless you,

Chapter One
Healing—is it God's will?

This question has been argued by many people over the years but the simple answer is **yes**. It is God's will for you to be healed and walk in health and enjoy your life and fulfil the destiny He has for you.

> **Beloved I pray that you may prosper in all things and be in health, just as your soul prospers.**
> 3 John 2

Jesus was moved with compassion

When someone is in pain the natural reaction or instinct is to help alleviate pain and so how much more God who loves with an unfathomable love would want to see His children free from pain. Our prime example is our Lord Jesus Christ: *'who went about doing good and healing all that were oppressed by the devil.'* (Acts 10:38)

Nowhere in the gospels did Jesus say no to healing; in fact He was always willing and ready to heal the sick and great multitudes followed Him. One thing you notice about Jesus is that *'He was moved with compassion.'* Always a great shepherd to the sheep, He fed the hungry and healed their sick. He even gave power to His disciples to go and heal the sick which they did (Matthew 10:1).

1

Healing is the children's bread

> For a certain woman, whose young daughter had an unclean spirit, heard of him, and came and fell at his feet: The woman was a Greek, a Syrophonician by nation: and she besought him that he would cast forth the devil out of her daughter. But Jesus said unto her, Let the children first be filled, for it is not good to take the children's bread, and to cast it unto the dogs. And she answered and said unto Him, Yes, Lord: yet the dogs under the table eat of the children's crumbs. And He said unto her, For this saying go thy way; the devil is gone out of thy daughter. And when she was come to her house, she found the devil gone out, and her daughter laid upon the bed.
>
> Mark 7:25-30

This is the only place Jesus refused healing, meaning that healing was provided for the children of Israel but under the Old Covenant the gentiles didn't have the right to receive healing. However, the gentile woman said: *"even the dogs eat of the crumbs that fall off the table"* - showing great faith and persistence.

Now we have become children of God we can know for sure that healing belongs to us. The bible is the final authority and as we read the life and works of Jesus we will be fully persuaded that it is His will for us to be healed. If it is His will for all to be saved from hell why would it not be His will for all to be healed?

Many people have not received healing and many have died, even good Christians have died sick and this is true but yet the scriptures cannot be broken.

> **Surely He has borne our griefs (*lit. sicknesses*) and carried our sorrows (*lit. pains*) Yet we esteemed Him stricken, smitten by God, and afflicted. But He was wounded for our transgressions; He was bruised for our iniquities. The chastisement for our peace was upon Him. And by His stripes we are healed.**
>
> Isaiah 53:4-5

This scripture is mentioned again in Matthew 8:17 i.e. Jesus is fulfilling Isaiah 53:4-5

> **He Himself took our infirmities and bore our sickness**
>
> Matthew 8:17

> **Who Himself bore our sins in His own body on the tree, that we, having died to sins, might live for righteousness, by whose stripes you were healed.**
>
> 1 Peter 2:24

Healing was purchased for us on the cross by Jesus and so we can receive healing for our bodies. Why some are not healed only God knows but that does not nullify the fact that it is His will for you and me to be healed. Again, God is no respecter of persons—if He heals one then He will heal another. God loves us all equally.

What about unbelievers?

The rain falls on the just and unjust and God's mercy extends not only to His children but to the whole world.

> **For God so loved the world that He gave His only begotten Son, that whoever believes in Him shall not perish.**
>
> John 3:16

Under the Old Covenant unbelievers could not expect anything from God but the New Covenant is for the whole world—whoever will believe.

God is Love

In reality, unbelievers are often the first to get healed. Many of them come expecting to receive healing and many come to Christ because of it. If God heals the unbeliever and the unjust how much more His own children. In our healing crusades we see Hindus, Muslims, Buddhists and New-agers getting instantly healed and some come to Christ.

Many of them come for the healing and not even for Jesus and yet the mercy of God extends towards them. God is love, the Bible says, and love cannot bear to see someone hurting or in pain.

> **So I say to you: Ask, and it shall be given to you; Seek and you will find; Knock and it will be opened to you.**
>
> Luke 11:9

Jesus went on to say,

If you then, being evil, know how to give good gifts to your children, how much more will your heavenly Father give the Holy Spirit to those who ask Him?

Luke 11:13

And so healing and salvation is available to whoever shall call upon Jesus, for He is no respecter of persons. In order to be fully persuaded in your own mind I would encourage you to read the gospels of Matthew, Mark, Luke and John and see the life and ministry of Jesus in operation.

Don't take anyone's word for it but find out for yourself. Jesus healed ALL who came to Him and it is His will for ALL to receive healing which He has provided through the cross.

Chapter Two
How to receive your healing

Some people find it very easy to receive their healing and some find it pretty difficult. Why this is so no-one knows except God. If you're very intellectual and want to figure it all out in your head first then you'll probably (and I'm saying probably) find receiving hard.

In Matthew 18:3 Jesus said, *"except you come as little children...."* Child-like faith is required in order to receive. Healing is a gift from God just like salvation. Usually I explain to people to receive healing just like they received their salvation which is receiving it first by faith. If the pain or symptoms leave then you're healed, but if they don't you are healed by faith but are trusting God for the manifestation.

Not everyone is healed instantly and for some it is a process of getting healed step by step. There are no formulas, though we love to have formulas but God will not be put in a box. **He wants to heal all** who come to Him and so we must look to Him at all times.

When the even was come, they brought unto him many that were possessed with devils: and he cast out the spirits with his word, and healed all that were sick.
                                                                        Matthew 8:16

Jesus healed the sick in so many different ways and this is because He was following the instructions of the Holy Spirit. This is why not everyone gets healed the same way and listening to the leading of the Holy Spirit is a major key as far as ministering healing to a sick person.

Confession

It is always good to come to God with a humble attitude and confessing your sins and forgiving those who have hurt you. This attitude puts you in a good position to receive. God resists the proud but gives grace to the humble in heart. Not that we need to beg or grovel to God in order to receive because this shows we don't know the love of God. God is love and He is our loving, heavenly Father. Not only did He give Jesus for our sins but also gave us His Holy Spirit to help us, comfort us and show us the way.

An atmosphere of belief

When the Holy Spirit is moving in a service and the presence of the Lord is evident many are able to receive. As we listen to testimonies of healing our faith is stirred and we can reach out and take healing from the Lord. On many occasions we have seen that when one person gets healed it triggers the faith of others also to receive. Other times we can keep going to healing meetings and sooner or later we too can receive, but again I emphasise - there are no formulas!

You can receive healing by the laying on of hands or just

sitting in a service, reaching out by faith to receive for yourself. In some cases people have been healed just being in a service and suddenly they realise their pain has gone or their growth has disappeared. This is why **we give all the glory to God because surely all healing comes from Him and Him alone.**

The word of knowledge

> **For to one is given by the Spirit the word of wisdom; to another the word of knowledge by the same Spirit**
>
> 1 Corinthians 12:8

Sometimes a minister will have a 'word of knowledge' which describes your situation or sickness and on such occasions it is best to receive it by faith and if the word is accurate healing will usually manifest. Words of knowledge help us to receive because we see God recognising our predicament and we are able to again receive. Also in that word there is enough faith and power for us to be healed.

The important thing is not to give up but to keep trusting the Lord. He is a God of great compassion and He loves all equally and has no favourites. What He has done for one, He will do for another. Some folks like to prepare by fasting and praying so that they can receive and this is good though not always necessary. There are many instances where people feel unworthy so that they can't receive but again healing (like salvation) is a free gift and it's got nothing to do with our worthiness. It is because (like salvation) healing was purchased for us on the cross.

Putting action to your faith

> **And as Jesus passed by, He saw a man which was blind from his birth……(v6) He spat on the ground, and made clay of the spittle, and he anointed the eyes of the blind man with the clay, and said to him, Go wash in the pool of Siloam…..he went his way therefore, and washed and came seeing.**
>
> John 9:1-7

When you believe God is healing you it is good to try to do something you couldn't do before, e.g. if you had back pain (which is very common) try bending slowly and see if the Lord indeed has touched you. One particular lady had arthritis in her whole body and in the prayer line she was prayed for three times but nothing happened.

Disappointed she hobbled back to her seat and as she sat down, suddenly all the arthritis left her body and she jumped up and started shouting and leaping for joy.

Undoubtedly heaven came down and many others were healed just by seeing her shout for joy! In Luke 6:10 Jesus asked the man with a withered hand to stretch forth his hand and as he did it was restored whole. For instance, if you have a hearing aid, take it off and see if you can hear without it, or if you're wearing glasses, take them off and check if you can see without them etc…

9

Other methods

You can receive also by someone anointing you with oil or in other cases you might have a spirit of infirmity cast out of your body. We will look at this later in the manual. Some folks have been known to obtain healing by listening to a healing programme on the radio or Christian TV or just praying a simple prayer of faith.

You can receive healing in so many different ways, for some it is instant and for others it is progressive. The important thing to know is God wants to heal you for God is love. It's like taking an aspirin for a headache; you don't put the tablet on your hurting head, instead you swallow it and the medication deals with the pain through the blood stream. In the same way you receive healing into your spirit and then that healing finds its way to your physical problem.

Chapter 3
Why are some not healed?

This is a very interesting question that many have tried to answer but the short answer is that only God alone knows everything about everyone. He alone knows what is going on in a person's life, where they are at and what is causing the problem. People get healed in many different ways and we cannot simply put healing in a box or formula and say this is how it works. You cannot throw the baby out with the bath water—just because someone does not got healed and dies or whatever does not mean that God does not desire to heal.

Unforgiveness

And when you stand praying, forgive, if you have ought against any: that your Father also which is in heaven may forgive you your trespasses. But if you do not forgive, neither will your Father which is in heaven forgive your trespasses.

Mark 11:25, 26

There was a lady I knew when I was pastoring a church who had terrible pain in her back which no doctor could do anything about. Every Sunday she came forward for healing but never got healed. She went to many healing conferences and special meetings but the pain remained.

She would come to me all the time for prayer and I too

grew weary and finally in desperation I asked the Lord why she could not receive her healing. The Lord whispered just one word to me - 'neighbour'. This word did not make much sense but that's what the Lord said.

The following Sunday she came again for prayer for healing and this time I said, "Maria, the Lord gave me a word for you—he says, 'neighbour'. The moment I said that she screamed out loud and got healed.

Naturally I was astonished and perplexed. She got so excited about her healing and explained how her neighbour troubled her every night with loud music and she couldn't forgive him. The Lord was dealing with her on unforgiveness but she adamantly refused to forgive her neighbour. Her healing came instantly when her sin or unforgiveness was revealed.

Unforgiveness will block your healing and it is very, very important to really forgive and release people who have hurt you. (Matthew 18:21-35) Just as you would release a caged bird—open up your heart and release all the unforgiveness out of your heart.

Lack of Faith?

Unforgiveness is a big issue in healing but not always. I've heard ministers say it's because of a lack of faith. Well actually it does not take much faith to be healed because people who say they have no faith at all have been healed. Others have been healed sitting in a crowd, noticing pain leaving their bodies and no-one has

12

touched them or prayed for them.

We have seen many healed without any prayer at all. So how is this happening? It is I believe a question of **receptivity.** Some individuals are very receptive to what is being offered whilst others don't know how to open their heart and receive the free gift of healing.

Concerning the blind man who sat by the way begging, Jesus asked him what He should do for him.

> **And he said, Lord, that I may receive my sight. And Jesus said to him, <u>Receive thy sight</u>: thy faith has saved thee.**
>
> Luke 18:41, 42

A feeling of unworthiness is a possible reason. Some Christians have been taught to muster up their faith but this is also wrong. Faith comes by hearing and hearing from God's word and when God speaks to our hearts faith is there in that word. However it does take faith to keep your healing and resist the devil who will try to rob you of your healing.

Gradual healing

Also many receive their healing gradually for not all healing is instant. Sometimes this can be a good thing as there are issues being sorted out in the process. But we cannot say God does not heal if some dear Christian dies without being healed. There is a reason but we don't always know why. It does hurt and we may feel somewhat confused but God is love and He is no respecter of persons.

It is not necessarily a lack of faith either. Another reason some do not receive their healing is due to a broken heart. (*'Hope deferred makes the heart sick'*—Proverbs 13:12) In eternity I guess we'll know everything. Once someone's emotions are healed (we call this inner healing) then the physical healing will manifest.

Casting out spirits of infirmity

> **And behold, there was a woman which had a spirit of infirmity eighteen years, and was bowed together, and could in no wise lift up herself. And when Jesus saw her, he called her to him, and said unto her, Woman, thou art loosed from thine infirmity. And he laid his hands on her, and immediately she was made straight, and glorified God.**
>
> Luke 13:11-13

Some need a curse broken or a spirit cast out before healing can manifest. A blind man was healed when we broke the curse over his life. Another who was dying of cancer had demons cast out of his body and he received healing. Much sickness is caused by evil spirits but not all sickness is spiritual. Knowing how to discern the cause of sickness is important.

Can a Christian have a demon people often ask me. A Christian cannot have a demon in his spirit because the Holy Spirit lives there, however a demon can live in his physical body in the form of sickness or in his mind as oppression and those demons need to be cast out.

Although demonic oppression is real we must be careful not to glorify the devil and his work. Neither should we attribute everything to the devil. No demon can remain when the presence of God is around. If we constantly talk about the devil and demons they will show up. Talk about Jesus and the devils will scatter.

Authority in His Name

In many cases we have seen healing manifest when a spirit is cast out. A person receiving this deliverance may cough or sigh or even yawn. In extreme cases vomiting may occur or shaking and screaming.

Naturally this can be frightening to those who are unaccustomed to it; however Jesus has given us the authority to cast out these spirits in His Name.

> **And these signs shall follow them that believe: In my name shall they cast out devils, they shall speak with new tongues. They shall take up serpents; and if they drink any deadly thing, it shall not hurt them; they shall lay hands on the sick and they shall recover.**
>
> Mark 16:17

Chapter 4
Can someone lose their healing?

This is a very important question and the answer is yes. For some reason certain people get healed and stay healed without any problem and yet there are others who have lost their healing. Receiving healing is sometimes easier than keeping it! Healing received by faith is spiritual and therefore if you don't know spiritual laws you can lose your healing. It's as if when you get saved, the devil will come and bring doubts to your mind and if you pay heed to those doubts you will feel you are not saved.

This is why new believers have to be taught not to walk by their feelings but rather to stand on the Word of God and walk by faith. I don't always feel married and yet I know I am because I have a ring on my finger and a marriage certificate. Usually you are asked to produce a certificate to prove your marriage because even though you are together you can't prove you are married without one.

Don't give the devil room

The devil is a thief and will try to steal your healing if you let him. Just as Peter walked on water but sank as he saw the wind and the waves, so we must keep our eyes on Jesus and not on any lying symptoms the devil may bring us.

When the unclean spirit is gone out of a man, he walks through dry places, seeking rest; and finding none, he says, I will return to my house whence I came out.

Luke 11:24

Neither give place to the devil

Ephesians 4:27

Also in healing a spirit may have been cast out and that spirit will try to return and so we need to stand fast in faith and resist the devil. I knew a lady with cancer and as I prayed for her I felt she needed to forgive her husband who had abused her for 26 years. She forgave him and was totally healed and the hospital cleared her as she had no trace of cancer.

Weeks later there was a dispute over some money and she took her husband to court. I warned her but she did not listen—rather she listened to her relatives who also hated her husband. The cancer came back and she eventually died.

A sad case, but we must remain vigilant and not allow anger, bitterness and unforgiveness to come into our hearts, thus giving the devil room. *Bless those that curse you and pray for them who despitefully use you* Jesus said (Matthew 5:44).

Taking authority

In prayer we make sure that spirit is not only bound but cast out and the person receiving the healing knows their authority in Christ and stands in faith concerning their healing.

Jesus said when he cast out the dumb and deaf spirit,

> **Thou dumb and deaf spirit, I charge thee, come out of him, and enter no more into him.**
>
> Mark 9:25

Also he instructed the man by the pool of Bethesda after He had healed him,

> **Behold thou art made whole: sin no more, lest a worse thing come unto thee.**
>
> John 5:14

It is very important to read the Word of God daily and be part of a strong fellowship of believers. This way you keep strong in faith i.e. faith is a shield which will ward off the fiery darts of doubt and unbelief (Ephesians 6:10-18)

Taking care of our bodies

Our bodies are the temple of the Holy Spirit and we are to properly take care of ourselves with exercise, proper nutrition, rest etc... Many are sick because they neglect to take care of their bodies. Just like a car it needs to be regularly serviced and maintained for longer service.

Our bodies are magnificently designed but they can only take so much. Modern diets are literally killing people because they lack the minerals and vitamins our bodies need.

Finally, a daily dose of God's word is needed so our spirits remain well fed and nourished. The word of God is like medicine to our bodies.

> **My son, attend to my words; incline your ear unto my sayings. Let them not depart from your eyes; keep them in the midst of your heart. For they are life to those that find them, and health to all their flesh.**
>
> Proverbs 4: 20-22

Resist the devil

Finally we cannot be passive in our faith but must aggressively resist the devil who tries to steal our healing if we let him. James 4:7 says, humble yourself before God and then resist the devil who will flee from you. We must always try to stay humble before God and then the devil will find it hard to fight us.

Chapter 5
Healing and the Word of God

The Word of God is the will of God revealed. Jesus is called the Word of God in John's gospel (John 1:1) and Jesus healed the sick everywhere He went. In Matthew, Mark, Luke and John Jesus is seen to heal multitudes. Since we are to be followers of Jesus and we are His disciples, we too are called to heal the sick.

The key is to have confidence that God wants to heal people. In fact healing, which is part of the atonement, is already provided for just like salvation. We simply appropriate what the Word of God declares is already provided for us.

The bible says *'my people are destroyed for lack of knowledge'* (Hosea 4:6). When we know what God's word has to say about healing then we will walk in understanding and revelation.

Jesus took the curse

In 1 Peter 2:24 the Bible says, *'by His stripes we are healed'* - past tense. Healing was provided by the stripes which were laid upon Jesus' back. In Galatians 3:13, 14 Jesus took the curse, and sickness and disease are part of the curse which Jesus bore.

Christ has redeemed us from the curse of the law, being made a curse for us: for it is written, Cursed is everyone that hangs on a tree: That the blessing of Abraham might come on the Gentiles through Jesus Christ; that we might receive the promise of the Spirit through faith.

Galatians 3:13, 14

The blessings and curses are clearly defined in Deuteronomy 28 and it is clear that sickness comes only under the curse. We don't need to tolerate sickness anymore but we can rebuke it in the Name of Jesus. A lot of sickness is caused by demons infesting people's bodies and so when they are cast out healing is manifested. For example, arthritis is a spirit of infirmity which needs to be cast out and even cancer which is a spirit of death can be cast out in Jesus' name.

Christians cannot be possessed because they are already the abode of the Holy Spirit, but these demons of sickness and disease can be living in the flesh or even sometimes the mind realm, i.e. oppression is a demon oppressing a believer's mind and needs to be resisted.

God's word is established

Meditating in the word of God is very important because faith comes from God's Word. Without faith we can do nothing because in the spiritual realm everything works through faith in God (Hebrews 11:6) and the finished work of Calvary.

In Matthew 4:4 Jesus said, *'man cannot live by bread alone'* and also He fought the devil with the word of God. We cannot fight the devil with our bare hands as he is a fallen angel but he will and must submit to the word of God.

God's word is established and is unmoveable, unshakeable and we can put our trust in His word because *what He has said will not return to Him void but is full of power.* (Isaiah 55:11)

Everything in the universe was created by the word of God. (Hebrews 11:3) In Genesis 1, God said it and it was. Jesus is the Word and the *Word became flesh and dwelt among us* (John 1:14). The word of God feeds our spirit man and makes us spiritually strong. In order to operate in healing we must feed on God's word daily.

Those believers who do not regularly feed on His word are weak and easily overcome by the devil's devices and temptations. When the anointed word of God is released it brings healing to our bodies. Sickness and disease will respond to the word of God and leave.

He sent His Word and healed them and delivered them from their destructions.

Psalm 107:20

Chapter 6
Healing and the Holy Spirit

The Word of God, the Bible, was written by men of God inspired by the Holy Spirit (2 Timothy 3:16). The Spirit of God stirred up those men and therefore we have the Holy Scriptures available to us.

Without the inspiration and unction of the Holy Spirit the word of God can be dry and difficult to absorb. Just like natural food requires moisture so the word of God needs the inspiration of the Holy Spirit for it to have power.

Knowing this first, that no prophecy of the scripture is of any private interpretation. For the prophecy came not in old time by the will of man: but holy men of God spoke as they were moved by the Holy Ghost.

2 Peter 1:20, 21

Faith comes by hearing, and hearing by the Rhema (as written in the original Greek) or quickened Word of God (Romans 10:17). When the Word of God is quickened by the Spirit of God, then this Word will have much power and accomplish much.

This is why there are many theologians and scholars who cannot understand or believe in the virgin birth or the miracles of Jesus. They are trying to understand the Word of God intellectually and without the help of the

Holy Spirit. The Spirit is the great teacher for He is the real author of the Bible. Also, since the Bible is a spiritual book we need the Holy Spirit to reveal its truths. It is very difficult to believe the Bible without the help of the Holy Spirit - He is the Spirit of Life and He brings life to the words we read.

Jesus worked with the Spirit

Also, healing is the work of the Holy Spirit. After Jesus was anointed by the Holy Spirit he began to perform the healings and miracles (Luke 4:18). Jesus had the help of the Holy Spirit. Whatever the Spirit told Him to do or say, Jesus obeyed and the miracles happened.

In Genesis 1 the Spirit of God was hovering and when God spoke the word, the Holy Spirit created the universe. The Holy Spirit heals people in many different ways and that is why we cannot simply copy one method of healing. We follow the leading of the Spirit as we operate healing and deliverance. Zech 4:6 declares, *'it's not by might, nor by power but by My Spirit, says the Lord'.*

We too need the anointing (or empowerment) of the Spirit to operate in healing and miracles (Acts 1:8). The Holy Spirit is a divine person and we need to learn to have fellowship with Him and obey His instructions. (2 Corinthians 13:14). He is the senior partner and we are the junior.

As we hear and obey His leading and speak the word of God, healing and miracles will be manifested, for without Him we can do nothing.

The Holy Spirit is not a dove or oil or wind but the third person of the Godhead. Also, He is easily grieved and so we must walk carefully in His presence. His nature is likened to a dove but yet He is incredibly powerful. Since Jesus has gone to heaven it is the Spirit we do business with. He is now orchestrating everything God desires on the earth and so in healing we must work with the Spirit of God. The work of God becomes effortless when we are totally dependent upon His power.

> **Howbeit when he, the Spirit of truth, is come, he will guide you into all truth: for he shall not speak of himself; but whatsoever he shall hear, that shall he speak: and he will show you things to come. He shall glorify me: for he shall receive of mine, and shall show it unto you.**
>
> John 16:13, 14

In 2 Corinthians 13:14 we are told to fellowship with Him and this is where we get to know Him. Sitting quietly in His presence is important so that we can hear His still small voice.

> **The grace of the Lord Jesus Christ, and the love of God, and the communion of the Holy Ghost, be with you all. Amen.**
>
> 2 Corinthians 13:14

The anointing (or empowerment) comes when we meditate in God's Word and fellowship regularly with the Holy Spirit. Many ministers are very busy in God's work but they neglect the important business of ministering to the Lord in worship, spending quality time with Him. In John 15:5 Jesus said that without Him we can achieve nothing but with Him we can do great things.

Chapter 7
The Gifts of the Holy Spirit

As the name implies, the gifts belong to the Holy Spirit and He distributes them as He wills. In 1 Corinthians, the twelfth chapter we see outlined all the nine gifts of the Spirit and they are given to the church to accomplish God's purpose on earth.

The Apostle Paul in 1 Corinthians 14:1 tells us to desire spiritual gifts, therefore it is God's will for us to operate and use the gifts to edify and build up His church.

> **For to one is given by the Spirit the word of wisdom; to another the word of knowledge by the same Spirit, To another faith by the same Spirit, to another the gifts of healing by the same Spirit, To another the working of miracles; to another prophecy, to another discerning of spirits, to another various kinds of tongues, to another the interpretation of tongues.**
>
> 1 Corinthians 12: 8-10

Many people in the church have been given gifts but either they are not aware of them or have not had a chance to exercise them. The local church or house group is a good place to start under the authority of the pastor or leader so that as Paul writes all may learn.

Obviously the more you work the gifts the better you get at using them and so - where do you begin? Practice makes perfect - but some are afraid to step out because of the fear of failure. As long as we remain humble and are prepared to make mistakes and even be corrected we can make progress. Gradually confidence will come and you will flow more easily in the gifts.

Knowing His voice

Since the gifts come from the Holy Spirit and the Spirit is a Person, we need to go to Him and ask and receive from Him. The gifts require primarily that we can know His voice and leading, therefore it is imperative we spend time in His presence on a daily basis. As we hear His voice (in our hearts and minds) or His promptings and we obey those promptings then we shall see His power being manifested. The Holy Spirit can easily be grieved (Ephesians 4:30) therefore we must work carefully and with a right attitude especially ensuring we give all the glory to God.

When the miracles start happening it is quite easy to believe that it had something to do with you, whereas without Him we can do nothing. We are simply the vessel and His is the power or anointing, or we are the wire (conduit) and He is the electricity. People have a tendency to exalt the preacher who has the gifts, not realising the gifts come from God. Anyone can operate in the gifts as long as they love the Lord and give all glory to Him.

Being open to the Spirit

Generally speaking we can operate in two or three gifts well and in others not as well. Some people are very exercised in one gift, for example, healing, and therefore people are often healed through them. Some are more proficient in prophecy and are quick to exercise this gift at a moment's notice.

One thing I have noticed is that some folks are more flexible and others are more reserved and less likely to move in the Spirit. He is described as a wind (which is flowing and unpredictable) and so the more open we are the better. There are always cases where some half-baked Christians think they are operating in the gifts but it is simply foolishness, imagination or pride. However, we must not throw the baby out with the bathwater so to speak!

Leaders who are more cautious or even afraid are less likely to see manifestations of the Spirit in their congregations and there are many people who are stifled. People everywhere are hungry and thirsty for the genuine move of the Spirit and more and more congregations of all denominations are opening up to this. There will always be wacky and foolish folks around but we seek after the real thing.

Quench not the Spirit. Despise not prophesyings. Prove all things; hold fast that which is good.
2 Thessalonians 5:19-21

Learning to discern

> Beloved, believe not every spirit, but try the spirits whether they are of God: because many false prophets are gone out into the world. Hereby know ye the Spirit of God: Every spirit that confesses that Jesus Christ is come into the flesh is of God: and every spirit that confesses not that Jesus Christ is come in the flesh is not of God....
>
> 1 John 4:1-3

I am naturally a suspicious person and am not quick to trust prophecies or 'words from the Lord' and this can be a healthy thing. Leaders need to be especially discerning as lives can be wrecked by some wacky Christians. How do you know what is God and what is either the devil or even your own mind? A good question and probably the most important.

> My sheep hear my voice, and I know them and they follow me
>
> John 10:27

Getting to know His voice and leading is a process during which you will make mistakes; however if it is in your heart to encourage and build up and you have a humble attitude it will work out well. Jesus was moved with compassion and healed the sick and that is the key—the compassion of God moves us to pray for those who are hurting **and the Lord (the Holy Spirit) will direct us.**

At first His voice will not be very clear but gradually as you 'step out' it will become more obvious. Stepping out in faith is where many believers miss out because of the fear of getting it wrong. You've got to take the bull by the horns and go for it; after all you've only got one life, and how long are you going to remain in the boat instead of walking out on the water (please not literally!).

Using the gifts is a lot of fun too and can bring tremendous encouragement to people who need a word or confirmation from the Lord. Jesus operated in the gifts continually and He knew what people were thinking too! He healed the sick, cast out devils using the discerning of spirits, used the word of knowledge and operated in the gift of faith and miracles. Many times several of the gifts are used simultaneously, e.g. the word of knowledge and healing go pretty much hand in hand.

Neglect not the gift that is in thee, which was given thee by prophecy.....

1 Tim 4:14

Wherefore I put thee in remembrance that thou stir up the gift of God, which is in thee by the putting on of my hands. For God has not given us the spirit of fear; but of power, and of love, and of a sound mind.

2 Tim 1:6, 7

Desire to help

How do you know which gift you've been given by the Lord? Again, only by use and what comes naturally to you is a good guide. Some believe that since we have the Holy Spirit we have all the gifts in us and this is true - however it is as He wills that the operation comes into being.

Again the hungrier you are the better and the desire to help and comfort people must be paramount. I always say have a go and see what happens. You cannot steer a stationary car, so put the foot on the gas and go with God and see what happens.

Finally, practice makes perfect and constant time with God and His Word, together with many opportunities will perfect the gifts. Don't be afraid of making mistakes and be open to correction from your leaders and all shall be well.

In my own case I always seem to have a second pair of eyes so to speak. I can see beyond the physical realm without really trying. Somehow I seem to know when people are getting healed or not and even see evil spirits as they come out of people—sometimes but not always. Gifts from God are gifts and as we desire them and ask God He will grant them to us.

Chapter 8
What to do if you're not healed the first time

It is true not everyone gets healed the first time they are prayed for and it can be discouraging and questions can arise. God has no favourites and He loves us all equally and healing is available to all but we are all in different places on our journey with God.

Probably the most important thing is to be persistent like the widow woman (Luke 18:5) or the woman with the issue of blood in Mark 5:25. This woman had spent all her money and was no better for it. She heard Jesus was healing multitudes and though the crowd was great she pressed though and touched the hem of Jesus' garment. Jesus turned around and said "who touched me?", and the disciples were amazed because a multitude was thronging Jesus and trying to touch Him, but the difference was that this woman touched Jesus believing and she was healed.

She believed so much that Jesus felt the power flow out of Him and knew that someone had touched Him with faith. Many people don't realise healing, (like salvation), is a free gift and we should receive it like a child or with child-like faith.

And shall not God avenge his own elect, which cry day and night to him, though he bear long with them? I tell you that He will avenge them speedily. Nevertheless when the Son of man comes, shall he find faith on the earth?

Luke 18: 7, 8

It is very important also to surround yourself with believing Christians who are strong in faith to stand with you and come into agreement with you for your healing. The last thing you want is to have people who spout out doubt and unbelief around you.

The Bible says we must fight the good fight of faith (1 Timothy 6:12) and for some it is a tough battle to obtain healing. For others healing comes quite easily, however those who battle through to receive healing are more likely to keep their healing because the devil will frequently try to steal it back. The enemy is a deceiver and his job is to deceive the believer and make him or her think there is something wrong. Either God does not love them enough or they have some secret sin or even that they don't have enough faith.

Continue to read the word of God on healing, listen to testimonies, pray and seek the Lord and continue to believe. Healing is for **all** who come to Jesus and whether you receive healing instantly or not, we must not give up!

The measure of faith

> For I say, through the grace given unto me, to every man that is among you, not to think of himself more highly than he ought to think; but to think soberly, according as God has dealt to every man <u>the measure of faith.</u>
>
> Romans 12:3

God has given all of us the measure of faith. Not having enough faith is a common misconception among believers, for it does not take much faith to be healed. It is the capacity to receive this free gift which is the real issue here, not how much faith you have.

Staying in praise and thanksgiving

The good thing that comes out during the waiting period is that God uses the time to deal with us and eventually the Christian who has been through the fiery furnace is a better Christian for it as the dross has been removed. Staying in an atmosphere of praise and thanksgiving is also vital because praise and thanksgiving will keep us believing and trusting God. A praising Christian will not have time to moan and complain and talk defeat. God is glorified with a sacrifice of praise and healing will come if we faint not.

> He (Abraham) staggered not at the promise of God through unbelief; but was strong in faith, giving glory to God...
>
> Romans 4:20

Perseverance

Healing can also come when we are in an atmosphere of faith such as a healing service. One young man who was in a wheelchair had been prayed for over 1400 times but there was no healing. He never gave up but kept asking for prayer and suddenly his healing came. He is now a very strong believer because his faith was tested the limit. Another woman I had prayed for who was in a wheelchair grabbed her crutches and was determined to walk, and throughout the whole service she kept hobbling along with her crutches with help from the pastor. Eventually she gave me the crutches and declared she didn't want them anymore and was considerably better. This is a fight of faith and we must persevere and keep Away From Doubting Thomases.

> **...Blessed are they that have not seen, and yet have believed.**
>
> John 20:29

> **...and so, after he (Abraham) had patiently endured, he obtained the promise.**
>
> Hebrews 6:15

Probably the best thing I recommend is to continuously pray and meditate and look at all the various healings Jesus did to increase your faith. Healing is like salvation—you don't have to beg God for it because salvation is already provided; it is simply a case of receiving salvation with a child-like faith. Healing is the same. **It is already provided.**

Chapter 9
The difference between hope and faith

This subject is very important and many folks find it difficult to understand the difference between hope and faith but it is vital we know it. Hope is always in the future whereas faith is always in the present. Hope says 'someday I will be healed', whereas faith says 'I receive my healing now'. The trouble begins when we don't receive our healing and we switch into hope.

> ....**What things soever ye desire when ye pray, believe that ye receive them and ye shall have them.**
>
> Mark 11:24

> **Now faith is the substance of things hoped for, the evidence of things not seen.**
>
> Hebrews 11:1

Healing, like salvation, is already provided for by God and so we simply receive by faith, and whether we see any change in our physical bodies or not we are receiving from Him. Hope says someday God is going to heal me when it suits Him or when He thinks I should be healed. God is always in the eternal present and everything we ever shall need including healing is already provided.

The key is to appropriate what He has already promised us. For example, radio waves are constantly being transmitted in the air but until our receiver—a radio or TV is hooked up in receive mode we will not see or hear anything. God is not going to heal us for He has already provided healing for us. We simply receive what He has already provided just like salvation. It's no use crying or begging because that does not make sense—rather, ask God to help you receive!

By His stripes you were healed

Salvation is probably easier to understand. He is not **going** to save the whole world for He has **already** provided salvation for the whole world through Jesus. If the whole world at the same moment or at any time receives the gift of salvation then they will be saved. God is not **going** to save the world - the world needs to recognise the finished work of the cross of Jesus. Similarly God is not **going** to heal you for healing was provided on the cross. 1 Peter 2:24 says, *'By His stripes you were healed* (past tense)'.

The difficulty is appropriating what is rightfully ours. It is no use thinking that God is going to heal you in the future for this is living in **hope** but let us think instead that God has provided healing for us so we believe that we receive it.

Mark 11:24 declares that we must believe we receive when we pray. We believe we have received before we see any manifestation. Many folks have received salvation and felt nothing but yet they are saved because they stand on God's promise. Healing is the same in that we believe before we see. Remember the fig tree Jesus cursed in Mark 11:14. It wasn't till the next day that the disciples noticed it had completely dried up from the roots. So continue to be prayed for and continue to receive healing and sooner or later the physical healing will manifest in your body.

Healing can be a process

Does this mean we do not receive any more prayer for healing if we have already been prayed for once? No! We continue to have hands laid on us and continue to intercede because healing also can be a process. This stand of faith becomes crucial when we need to learn to keep our healing. A lady in one of my meetings stood in front of me while I was ministering healing and all the pain left her knees.

Ten minutes later the pain returned and she came forward for healing again. Her church had not taught her how to keep her healing. When we receive salvation the devil will come and tell us that we are not saved especially when we have sinned. However we learn to stand on the Word of God and we understand that we are saved whether we feel saved or not.

It's like getting married. On the wedding day we feel tremendously married but a week, month or year later the feelings are not there. We then look at the ring on our finger or the marriage certificate and know we are married for better or worse. Words were spoken in faith and a miracle took place in the spirit realm and two people became one.

Recovery

...they shall lay hands on the sick and <u>they shall recover.</u>

Mark 16:18

This scripture declares that the sick shall recover. Sometimes recovery takes a while but it doesn't mean that the process of healing hasn't started. Salvation and healing are the same. We stand on God's word regardless. Talking to the two lepers, Jesus said, 'Go, show yourselves to the priests...

...and it came to pass, that, <u>as they went,</u> they were cleansed.

Luke 17:14

A man I know suffered for many years and was waiting for the manifestation of his healing but it didn't come. I told him to believe that he had received and to stop waiting for the manifestation. He did that and the healing came. What was the difference? Previously he was living in hope and not in faith. He also kept saying that God was going to heal him (sometime in the future). Instead we should say, 'thank you Lord, healing is already provided and I continue to receive healing from you.'

Chapter 10
The person ministering must have faith

Two people are involved in healing—one receiving the healing and the other delivering healing. We always seem to concentrate our attention on the person receiving healing more than the minister of healing. However, it is very vital that the person delivering the healing gift has strong faith too! How can we have strong faith?

Faith comes by hearing, and hearing by the Word of God.

Romans 10:17

I believe it is imperative that the servant of God spends time daily reading the scriptures especially the verses pertaining to healing. Matthew, Mark, Luke and John, the four gospels, are full of healing in the ministry of our Lord Jesus. A lot can be learnt and absorbed reading all the accounts of healing in the gospels.

Also all the accounts of healing in the book of Acts. Paul and Peter both were used by God to heal the sick together with the other apostles like John and Phillip the evangelist. Reading and meditating daily on these accounts will build your faith, for until you are fully persuaded about healing there won't be much faith.

Peter and John at the hour of prayer in Acts 3 said, *'silver and gold have I none, but what I have I give to you. In the Name of Jesus, rise up and walk!'* The man who was crippled jumped up and walked. A great miracle happened and the place was in an uproar. Peter and John had strong faith and they used their faith to pray for the man.

> **And His name through faith in His name has made this man strong, whom you see and know: yes, the faith which is by Him has given him this perfect soundness in the presence of you all.**
>
> Acts 3:16

The anointing destroys the yoke

> **And it shall come to pass in that day, that his burden shall be taken away from off thy shoulder, and his yoke from off thy neck, and the yoke shall be destroyed because of the anointing.**
>
> Isaiah 10:27

Secondly, we must pray for the anointing which is God's divine enabling. As we pray in English and in tongues God will anoint us for His work. For without His anointing we can have no power.

In Luke 4 Jesus said, *'The Spirit of the Lord is upon me for He has anointed me to heal the sick....'* When we pray and seek the Lord the Holy Spirit will come and rest upon us.

This enabling is called the anointing and it is this anointing which destroys the yoke of oppression, sickness and disease.

> **How God anointed Jesus of Nazareth with the Holy Ghost and with power: who went about doing good and healing all that were oppressed of the devil; for God was with him.**
>
> Acts 10:38

Command sickness to leave

Thirdly, we need to step out and put into practice what we've learnt, i.e. look for opportunities to pray for the sick. We don't pray and say 'Lord please heal so and so' for He has already provided the healing on the cross.

Instead we say 'In the Name of Jesus, be healed!', or 'receive your healing in His Name' and deliver the healing by the laying on of hands or simply command the sickness to leave. Such as we have we give to the sick.

God has already done His part and now it is our job to take God at His word, believe that He has already made provision and administer the healing to the people. Too many believers are still praying 'O Lord, please heal so and so' and this prayer is incorrect. The healing virtue is already in us by the Holy Spirit and we impart it to whoever needs it.

Now this may not be easy to understand but this is praying in faith and not in hope - you will see more results if you believe God has already provided healing and so we minister healing to people by faith. As we believe and people receive with open hearts, healing will manifest.

Again, just as we minister salvation we do not say, 'Lord, save so and so...' when they are already ready to be saved. Instead we minister salvation by helping them pray the sinner's prayer and they receive salvation. Just as we minister salvation in His Name we also minister healing.

Chapter 11
What about Doctors?

The wisdom and knowledge that doctors possess comes from God and at the end of the day the purpose is to get well and whether you get well with the help of a doctor or not does not really matter. It is not good to run to the doctor every time you face minor medical problems as it is good practice to use your faith and trust God to heal you. Some people have more faith in the doctor's verdict than God's Word, but when medicine fails God is always there. God never fails, but we can fail in not trusting Him to fix our problems.

Modern medicine seems to focus a lot on the physical aspects of the sickness and doctors are sometimes reluctant to address the root causes. In many cases they are not taught on these aspects unlike the old days when a doctor who was a practising Christian would probably look to the Lord as well as his own knowledge to solve a problem.

A merry heart does good like a medicine: but a broken spirit dries the bones.

Proverbs 17:22

For example, deep felt resentment, anger and bitterness, if not dealt with through prayer and forgiveness will lead to all kinds of physical ailments like ulcers, arthritis, diabetes and even cancer. Doctors do not or may not be allowed to dwell in such areas, such a pity. They do however tell you about stress or diet and exercise which are very important indeed.

Medication

Sometimes people get confused about taking medication after prayer and this has caused some real problems. For instance, maybe you have diabetes and that insulin injection is keeping you alive. Maybe you get prayed for and believe you have received your healing. Please check it out with your doctor before you neglect to take your insulin shots. If you have received your healing the results will be confirmed!

This is particularly important in the case of serious illnesses. In the area of cancer and chemo-therapy the doctors may say for you to continue treatment but you may feel it unnecessary. In such cases decisions have to be made prayerfully. In the multitude of counsellors there is wisdom and talking it over with a number of doctors and your church leadership is helpful. At the end of the day it is not about stopping medication, it is knowing in your heart that God has healed you.

Spirit, mind and body

The bible teaches us that we have a spirit, a mind and a body and these three are intertwined. The bible also teaches us not to be quick to anger (Ecclesiastes 7:9).

Be ye angry and sin not: let not the sun go down on your wrath.

Ephesians 4:26

That is, deal with your anger and related issues before retiring for the night. When we suppress anger eventually there will be an explosion somewhere and these sorts of things are not discussed in the surgery. GPs are usually extremely busy and cannot spare the time to discuss your life in detail so they generally prescribe medication, but medication alone is insufficient.

To reset a bone you will need a trained person but the healing of that limb comes only from God. Doctors cannot heal anyone but they help the healing process through medication. The pharmacies are full of medicine bottles and yet we have more sick people today than ever before. The production and sale of medication is a multi-billion dollar business and therefore the more sick people the more money goes into someone's pocket.

Five a day

What, know ye not your body is the temple of the Holy Ghost which is in you, which ye have of God, and ye are not your own? For ye are bought with a price: therefore glorify God in your body, and in your spirit, which are God's.

1 Corinthians 7:2

Our bodies are the temple of God and so we must look after them, especially as they have to last us all our lives. A poor diet is probably one of the biggest issues facing us today when a third of a nation's population is considered obese. The modern diet which is packaged and convenient is killing many folks and there seems no end in sight. The pundits tell us that we should drink 8 glasses of water per day, 5 portions of fruit and vegetables (in America they have amended that to 8 portions) and half an hour of exercise per day.

These figures are accepted by most these days but people still prefer to drink soft drinks laced with sugar and other additives and other fast foods because we are so busy working that there is no time to prepare food the old fashioned way. The fast pace of life, the stress, and simply trying to cope from day to day is more than enough for people to deal with, but we need to slow down.

A simpler lifestyle is necessary with a few less material things to clutter our lives. People overeat because sometimes they are depressed, anxious or bored, and an adjustment in lifestyle is required for a healthier life. This is why time spent with God in His Word and also ministering to Him in praise and worship will help us to be less stressful, worried and have a healthier life. God's Word is medicine to our bodies and doctors now agree that people who have faith in God get better much quicker than those without faith.

Exercise

.......but I keep under my body, and bring it into subjection....

1 Corinthians 9:27

Many people need the motivation of a slimming group and I've heard many testimonies of weight loss using this method. Less meat and more fish and vegetables are recommended or perhaps a vegetarian diet may not be such a bad idea. We need to have a good look in our shopping trolleys and see if we cannot make some adjustments. If the weather is lousy then an exercise bike or stepper may be a good idea for those cold winter months. I usually use the stairs for my exercise and you can be puffing strongly in a few minutes of climbing stairs.

There really is no excuse but to get off our butt and do something and little changes everyday will eventually result in a new lifestyle. Reach for a glass of water instead of that soft drink—that's where you can start if you haven't already.

Sometimes a good scare and visit to the hospital with a look from a doctor saying you're not very well can be enough to get us going in the right direction. As you get older the problems can increase—it's like an old car which will need more maintenance and careful driving for a longer life. When you're young you can bounce back and young people care less but when you're older, the bones and joints need a regular dose of cod liver oil to keep them moving! For colds and flu, lots of fruit, vegetables and 1000 mg doses of Vitamin C are a great help I have found.

Prevention

Doctors are good and they are there to help, but prevention is better than cure! Doctors can give you a report to say there is no cure for cancer but with God nothing is impossible. However, you cannot abuse and neglect your body and expect divine health to function. No, our bodies are the temples of the Holy Spirit and God expects us to take care of them. (1 Corinthians 6:19)

'You are what you eat' someone once said and laziness is a poor excuse. People tell me they have no time to read their Bibles or even pray and yet they have three to four hours daily to watch television!

Chapter 12
Healing and Evangelism

Our greatest example is our Lord Jesus and to see what He did in the four gospels. He preached, He taught, He healed the sick and fed the hungry. Healing and the gifts of the Spirit are very instrumental when it comes to evangelism. The greatest miracle is when a person is born-again for you can get physically healed but still go to hell if you don't put your trust in Jesus' death and resurrection.

At the same time healing is like the dinner bell. It draws saints and sinners alike and we see how many thousands are born-again and healed in some major crusades, e.g. in Reinhard Bonnke's ministry the aim is for salvation but healing and miracles are what draw the crowd. Signs and wonders of healing and other miracles authenticate the gospel and people can see and experience the manifest presence of God in their midst. It is simply not enough to preach the Word, for opportunity must be given to the Holy Spirit to move among sick bodies and the gospel comes then not only in word but also in demonstration.

> ......and my speech and my preaching was not with enticing words of man's wisdom, but in demonstration of the Spirit and of power.
>
> 1 Corinthians 2:4

The God of miracles is still around

In the third world countries where there are few hospitals and the people are poor they look readily to God for a miracle as that's all they can have. They cannot buy the medicines they need so they put their trust in God's healing power. In the affluent west we have access to free medical care and subsequently we are not as desperate as poor people in the third world.

Also in the west, people are educated but not encouraged to have faith and therefore unbelief is prevalent. It takes a real moving of the Spirit with much prayer back-up to see the miraculous but it is happening now in the west. We are no longer satisfied with eloquent teachers who explain away healing and the gifts of the Spirit. Some have taught that the age of miracles passed away with the apostles; however the God of miracles is still around!

> **Jesus Christ the same, yesterday, and today and forever**
>
> Hebrews 13:8

Now, more than ever we need the supernatural to confound the sceptics!

When an unbeliever is in pain and the doctors are not able to help, they will be open to prayer. Here God can intervene and demonstrate His love and power and people will come to faith in Christ. Also, how can the sceptic differentiate between the religions of the world? Other religions say the same sort of thing about doing good etc., but when the presence and the power of the Lord is manifest, he or she will bow to Jesus very quickly. Healing therefore becomes a great tool for evangelism - but many folks are too scared and the fear of failure stops many from stepping out to pray for someone.

I always say that I am not the Healer, Jesus is, so if nothing happens don't blame me and that takes the pressure and focus off me. I tell people to look to Jesus for He is the Healer and He has already made provision for our healing so we can go to Him and receive. It's really as simple as that.

Multitudes

And great multitudes came unto Him, having with them those that were lame, blind, dumb, maimed, and many others, and cast them down at Jesus' feet: and He healed them: Insomuch that the multitude wondered, when they saw the dumb to speak, the maimed to be whole, the lame to walk, and the blind to see: and they glorified the God of Israel.

Matthew 15:30, 31

Why did great multitudes follow Jesus? If He was simply an eloquent speaker, He would have drawn only some people but Jesus was constantly surrounded by thousand trying to receive healing from Him. Signs and wonders do draw a crowd indeed and then they will listen to what you have to say.

Chapter 13
Healing and Deliverance

I met a man who was dying of cancer and everyone had prayed for him to no avail. It seems everything possible had been tried but there was no change. I was asked to pray for him also and the moment I did I saw (in the spirit) three demons in his body. I told the man that this was the reason for the cancer and so we cast these demons out in Jesus' Name and the man was instantly healed. How did we know that he was healed? Well, the pain left immediately and he didn't need the morphine anymore.

This man was a believer and yet the demons had entered him. Demons cannot possess a believer in Christ but they can afflict the believer with sickness or oppress him with things like depression etc... I don't look for demons in every corner as some do, and if you're not careful you can get into a real state and see demons even in your own shadow! This type of teaching of demonology is very dangerous but yet these demons are real and need to be dealt with.

Every knee must bow

I always emphasise the presence of Jesus and in His presence there is fullness of joy and there is no fear. The devil is no match for Jesus and he also is a defeated foe, who, by the way trembles at the very sound of the name of Jesus (James 2:19). Some believers seem to magnify the devil unwittingly and are always talking about what the devil is doing. No, rather let us talk about what the Lord is doing and give no glory to the devil. People who are brought up in superstition and such like are more prone to giving the devil undue credence when there is no power greater than the Lord's.

> **Wherefore God also has highly exalted Him and given Him a name which is above every name: That at the name of Jesus every knee should bow, of things in heaven, and things in earth, and things under the earth. And that every tongue should confess that Jesus Christ is Lord, to the glory of God the Father.**
>
> Philippians 2:10, 11

Jesus was always healing and casting out spirits of deafness (Luke 11:14) and dumbness with His word. He gave the devil no room to speak but simply cast them out and the people were healed. Sickness is not from God but from the devil so when the demons are cast out healing follows. Again, we do not spend hours and hours in this but as we function under the anointing of the Holy Spirit the work is done quickly and speedily.

> **Behold I give unto you power to tread on serpents and scorpions, and over all the power of the enemy: and nothing shall by any means hurt you.**
>
> Luke 10:19

Breaking curses

Not all sickness is demonic though some don't believe that. Many times we need to get people into a place where they can obtain their healing. Bad diet, lack of exercise and an unhealthy lifestyle all contribute to sickness and disease. God has given us an immune system which is there to protect us from sickness and disease but we need to take care of our immune system. It's a bit like the ozone layer which is slowly but surely being destroyed by too much carbon emission, i.e. too many cars burning fuel on the roads.

The rule of thumb is if a person is not getting healed then there may be a devil lurking which needs to be cast out. Also curses are passed down through the generations which need to be broken, e.g. if more than one member of the family has cancer or suffers from deafness then this could be a curse which needs to be broken, and we break the curses in the name of Jesus.

Fear not

> **And having spoiled principalities and powers, he made a show of them openly, triumphing over them in it (the cross).**
>
> Colossians 2:15

Finally, we must not be afraid of demons for they have been defeated by Jesus and since we have been given His name to use, the spirits will obey that Name. At the end of the day we must follow the leading of the Holy Spirit and seek God for the gift of the discerning of spirits. Time spent with the Holy Spirit on a daily basis is necessary to cultivate this relationship. He, the Holy Spirit, has all the answers and knows all things and He will show us what to do as we lean on Him.

Chapter 14
Different methods of healing the sick

The most common method is by the laying on of hands because we are taught in the bible to lay hands on the sick (Mark 16:18). And yet many people have been known to be healed without hands being laid upon them, i.e. Someone can be healed in a service just enjoying the presence of God and finding the pain has lifted. In one meeting of a famous evangelist a young Muslim boy heard God speak to him in an open-air crusade. He testified that a voice spoke to him several times to get up because he was healed, and as he did he was miraculously healed. In our meetings many have been healed just sitting in the service and some have been healed waiting in a prayer line. One lady who had a growth on her neck testified that she was healed on her way to the service and by the time she got to the meeting hall the growth had almost disappeared.

The gifts of healing

Is any sick among you? Let him call for the elders of the church: and let them pray over him, anointing him with oil in the name of the Lord: And the prayer of faith shall save the sick, and the Lord shall raise him up, and if he has committed sins, they shall be forgiven him.

James 5:15

In James we see that one way to receive healing is through the elders of the church anointing with oil. There is nothing special about the oil but it can be used as a point of contact and the oil signifies the work of the Holy Spirit. Then in 1 Corinthians 12:9 we are told of the gifts of healing. Some people are especially gifted by the Lord to operate in healing, however any believer can pray for someone who has a need. Many are healed through the word of knowledge and this is a wonderful gift because it helps the recipient to release their faith and grasp the healing.

For countless others healing is a process and they are gradually healed through repentance, forgiveness and walking in their healing day by day. Not everyone is instantly healed—of course this would be really great, however God is always dealing with issues concerning our hearts and our walk with him.

Getting others to pray

In many cases it is good to have people interceding on your behalf. It is much easier for someone else to believe for you than to believe for yourself. In serious emergencies when people have started round the clock prayer chains, life and death situations have resulted in miracles. Some people need to have a spirit of infirmity cast out of their bodies and healing will manifest as a result.

Chapter 15
Hindrances to receiving healing

Perhaps the greatest hindrance to receiving healing is that of not knowing whether God wants to heal you. Somehow we can believe God wants to heal someone else, but when it comes to believing for ourselves it's not so simple. Part of the reason can be low self-esteem and self-worth. The feeling of somehow not being good enough and this stems from a lack of knowledge of who God really is and how He works.

Sometimes our perception of God is altered because we may not have a loving earthly father and so trying to imagine a loving heavenly Father is difficult.

> **And behold, there came a leper and worshipped Him, saying, Lord, if thou wilt, thou canst make me clean. And Jesus put forth His hand, and touched him, saying, <u>I will</u>: <u>be thou clean</u>. And immediately his leprosy was cleansed.**
> Matthew 8:2, 3

The other hindrance to receiving is basically not knowing how to receive, i.e. when you are being prayed for it is no use just waiting to be zapped by God—receiving is an active mode and not a passive one. The action of opening your hands in expectation can help you receive. Healing is received by faith into your spirit, i.e. when you have a headache and you take an aspirin you don't put the aspirin on your head. Instead you swallow it and it goes into your blood stream, locates the pain and brings relief. Similarly you receive healing into your spirit through faith and it goes and relieves the pain.

An attitude of 'if God wants to heal me, He will and if not, He won't' is a major obstacle to receiving. On the contrary we must be positively aggressive in knowing that God wants to heal and He will heal us through His provision in the New Covenant and we simply need to learn to appropriate what Jesus purchased for us. The prayer 'if it be Thy will' is a prayer of consecration and concerns the direction God wants to take us in our lives.

A lack of knowledge, bad teaching, a negative attitude, are all hindrances to receiving your healing.

The unchanging Word

Forever O Lord, Thy word is settled in heaven.
Psalm 119: 89

Another block is when you hear of others who may have been hospitalised or even died and so a negative mindset can hinder us from receiving. Other people's experiences (positive and negative) do not negate the Word of God which is never changing, and Jesus is the same yesterday, today and forever.

And so don't go by other people's failures and ideas but go simply by the Word of God. Negative friends and relatives can greatly hinder our receptivity and so we must surround ourselves with strong like-minded people who believe God's Word and stand with us.

Forgive

> **Let all bitterness, and wrath, and anger, and clamour, and evil speaking, be put away from you, with all malice: And be ye kind one to another, tender-hearted, forgiving one another, even as God for Christ's sake has forgiven you.**
>
> Ephesians 4:31

Unforgiveness, anger, bitterness and resentment are great obstacles to receiving. We must forgive and release people so our hearts are soft and pliable to receive from the Lord. To forgive others is paramount if we are ever to receive healing for ourselves. Just like the bible says in Mark 11:25,26, *'When you stand praying forgive if you have ought against any, that your heavenly Father also which is in heaven may forgive you your trespasses—but if you do not forgive neither will your Father which is in heaven forgive your trespasses.'*

The scripture is very clear that God who has forgiven us so much expects us also to forgive. It's not always easy to forgive, for some wounds are so deep it takes the grace of God to do it, but do it we must. Unforgiveness only hurts the person holding it and many times the culprit is unaffected or may not even be aware of the damage he or she has caused. Unforgiveness is a poison which if not dealt with brings much hurt and pain including physical ailments. Though it is difficult, the fruit of forgiveness is sweet and we find much freedom. We become better and not bitter people—you might know of someone who has been bitter for decades and it has poisoned their whole lives and it's just not worth it.

Discerning the Lord's body

Forgiveness brings a unique release and we find healing comes because the door is shut to the enemy and he has no more authority to bring sickness to our bodies. Not only do we forgive but also we must ask God to forgive us. When we break God's laws, or walk in disobedience it gives the devil room to attack and God cannot then protect us. In 1 Corinthians 11 at the time of breaking bread we are told to examine and judge ourselves so that we do not get sick.

> **But let a man examine himself, and so let him eat of the bread and drink of the cup. For he who eats and drinks in an unworthy manner eats and drinks judgment to himself, not discerning the Lord's body. For this reason many are weak and sick among you, and many sleep.**
>
> 1 Corinthians 11:28-30

We constantly need to forgive and receive forgiveness and healing will come as our hearts are humbled and we become more pliable.

Go for it!

Among some English people there is also a reservation or an attitude of 'I don't want to bother God' which also hinders receptivity. When a word of knowledge is given but not acted upon, it will benefit no-one, and shyness or being reserved must not be allowed to get in the way of our healing. This again stems from a low self-worth—an attitude than says 'it must be for someone else and not for me.'

> **And from the days of John the Baptist until now the kingdom of heaven suffers violence, and the violent take it by force.**
>
> Matthew 11:12

Chapter 16
Having a positive attitude

Faith is the opposite of fear and as faith comes by hearing the Word of God (Romans 10:17) so also fear comes by hearing negative or evil reports.

Guard thy heart with all diligence: for out of it are the issues (forces) of life.

Proverbs 4:23

The heart here means spirit. Guard your spirit man. How can we guard our hearts? The eyes and ears are the entrance to our hearts. What we see and hear enters our inner being and creates negative or positive images or mindsets. Secondly, what we say continuously affects our spirit because we tend to believe what we say more than what others say. What we hear, what we see and say are the key elements which can create in us a positive or negative attitude. This is not done overnight, but over a period of time. If you don't pay attention to what you see, hear or say, you will have a negative attitude.

The world, especially the News is all negative. There is no such thing as a 'Good News Channel'. All News is negative, bad and full of calamities. As we meditate in God's Word daily and speak what God says, we create, over time a more positive attitude.

Speak positively

....God, who gives life to the dead and calls those things which do not exist as though they did;
Romans 4:17

If you meditate on healing scriptures you will have more faith for healing, however if you continuously ignore God's Word on healing and watch TV programmes especially hospital dramas you will become fearful. Fear is a spirit and we must guard our hearts against it. If you have cancer, don't think about your funeral or have images of dying because they do say many people die simply from fear rather than the disease. Fear is a killer and it will freeze your faith if allowed unchecked.

People wait until they are sick before turning to healing scriptures when sometimes it can be rather late in the day. No, immunise yourself daily with positive words from God, speak positively as much as possible and stay away from negative people. Stick around people who are positive and strong in faith, because people do influence us a great deal.

Do not meditate on pictures of doom and gloom - instead, visualise your healing—see yourself getting better! What you see and say eventually you will possess.

Expect good things

Many years ago I used to say 'Oh, I always get the flu around Christmas' and every Christmas I would get the flu. I was using faith but in a negative way. Now I stop using words and images of that kind, rather, I immunise myself with positive words, take Vitamin C, exercise and resist colds and flu on a daily basis.

Becoming positive or negative takes time, although becoming negative requires little effort, but becoming a positive person is going against the tide and it is hard but worth it. When praying for others we need to be positive and believe that they shall be healed - not just hope something will happen. Being positive is being expectant. Expect to be healed and expect others to be healed when you pray for them. Finally, watch your mouth, your eyes and your ears for these are the entrance into your heart.

Chapter 17
Believers shall lay hands on the sick

In Mark 16:18 Jesus spoke these words and said, *"believers shall lay hands on the sick and they shall recover"*. The Holy Spirit is given to all believers; therefore all believers can pray for the sick and see results. The ministry of healing is not for just the chosen few but it is for **all those who will believe God**. Anyhow, there are too many sick people and millions of unsaved and therefore we need all believers to be involved.

There are men and women of God who are His instruments and who have the gifts of healing operating through them in a much greater measure but this should not stop the ordinary believer from praying for the sick. After all, great men of God are very busy leading campaigns, travelling and not easily available and therefore we need the healing ministry at a local level. God is no respecter of persons and He will use anyone willing to pay the price.

> **And as you go preach, saying, The kingdom of heaven is at hand. Heal the sick, cleanse the lepers, raise the dead, cast out devils: freely you have received, freely give.**
>
> Matthew 10:7, 8

Believers who want to operate in healing must spend time getting to know the Holy Spirit and also to spend time meditating on healing scriptures. There are many who wish to operate the gifts but are unwilling to do their homework.

Jesus was moved by compassion, and that is the primary reason for healing, i.e. people are in pain and are hurting. There is nothing worse than to see a child suffering from cancer.

Prayer

Believers also need to spend much time in prayer—not begging God to heal for this is an insult to the character of God who is the God of love. For God so loved the world He gave His Son and since He has given His Son how will He not give us all things? Luke 11 says, *"if you who are evil* (in comparison to God) *give good gifts unto your children, how much more will your heavenly Father give you His Spirit."*

No, we spend time in prayer - or rather praying in the Spirit, for as we pray in the Spirit we build up our faith (Jude 20). As we are fervent in prayer and spending quality time with the Holy Spirit and His Word we shall be equipped and ready to minister healing. God is in us therefore healing can flow through our hands.

The disciples prayed for boldness, signs and wonders:

> **And now, Lord, behold their threatenings: and grant unto thy servants, that with all boldness they may speak thy word, by stretching forth thine hand to heal: and that signs and wonders may be done by the name of thy holy child Jesus.**
>
> Acts 4:29, 30

The disciples' prayer was answered mightily:

> **And with great power gave the apostles witness of the resurrection of the Lord Jesus: and great grace was upon them all.**
>
> Acts 4:33

Mix faith with your prayer

The bible tells us to lay hands on the sick and believe and expect pain to go. Many believers lay hands on the sick and then 'hope' that something will happen and so they don't mix faith with their prayer. The prayer of faith will move mountains, however the more we practise the better we get—at first if you don't see results, don't give up! Sooner or later someone will get healed and your faith will grow. Practice makes perfect and so find someone who is in pain and pray for them.

Even if you are afraid, do it while you're afraid for when you are weak then you are strong because you will be more dependent on the Holy Spirit.

Chapter 18
Authority of the believer and the Name of Jesus

As believers we have been given authority over the devil and all his works. We can and must use this authority to destroy the works of the devil and we do this by using the Name of Jesus (Philippians 2:9-11). The devil is a defeated foe for Jesus defeated him when He rose from the grave and took the keys of hell and death. The demons tremble at the sound of the Name of Jesus and they obey if you exercise faith in that mighty Name.

> **Jesus came and spake unto them saying, All power is given unto me in heaven and in earth, Go therefore......**
>
> Matthew 28:18

Jesus commands us to go in His Name and preach the gospel, heal the sick and cast out devils. We are His hands and feet and His mouthpiece, i.e. we are His Body and He is the Head of the Body. We are building His Kingdom in His Name and by the power of His Holy Spirit.

Resist the devil

The Name of Jesus cannot just be used any old how, i.e. some men tried that and the demons cried, *"Jesus we know, Paul we know, but who are you? And the demons prevailed upon the people"* (Acts 19:15).

But true believers have nothing to fear as long as they are submitted to the Lord. The bible says we are to humble ourselves under the mighty hand of God and then resist the devil and He will flee from us. Even the youngest and weakest believer has authority over the devil simply because the devil fears Jesus. (James 4:7)

> **Notwithstanding in this rejoice not, that the spirits are subject unto you; but rather rejoice, because your names are written in heaven**.
>
> Luke 10:20

The Name above every other name

For example, a policeman in his proper uniform can stop a ten truck lorry on the road because the driver of the truck recognises the authority of the uniform. He knows the uniform represents all the power of the government and the armed forces and therefore he will obey. But if you try to stop vehicles without the uniform you stand a good chance of being run over or locked up as a lunatic.

The Name of Jesus and the blood of Jesus is that uniform of heaven we wear and when the devil sees the blood and hears the Name of Jesus he obeys. Sickness and disease also have to obey because anything that is named in heaven or earth or under the earth is subject to the Name of Jesus.

In light of this we must use the Name of Jesus boldly and bring healing and deliverance to the afflicted.

Verily I say unto you, whatsoever you shall bind on earth shall be bound in heaven and whatsoever you shall loose on earth shall be loosed in heaven.

Matthew 18:18

Let us bind the works of the devil and set the captives free. Let us use our authority that God has given the church.

Chapter 19
Does God use sickness to reprove - and what about Job?

This probably is one of the most controversial subjects in the church and probably greatly misunderstood. First of all, God is a loving heavenly Father who is more loving and caring than any earthly father. Now let's think about this. No earthly father wants to or can bear to see his children suffer sickness so how can God put sickness on us to reprove us? It's like this—on earth when we disobey our parents and do harmful things we suffer the consequences.

In the same way when we do not obey God's laws then we suffer the result until we repent and turn back to God. He is a just and righteous God and therefore He has to allow judgement to fall when we break His laws.

The character of Jesus

This is why Jesus came, to fulfil all the law and in Jesus we are free. Not free to sin but when we do sin we have an advocate with the Father (1 John 2:1). In Jesus we find mercy and forgiveness, healing and deliverance. Jesus is the Son of God and He said, *"if you've seen me you've seen the Father"*. In other words, Jesus and God the Father are One and so to know what God is like we look to Jesus who is the very image of God.

Who being the brightness of His glory, and the express image of His person, and upholding all things by the Word of His power…..
Hebrews 1:3

Now Jesus never put sickness on anyone to reprove them but instead He healed **all** who came to Him without exception. The only way we can comprehend God is by looking at Jesus. And so we confuse ourselves when we see children dying of cancer—God did not do that and He did not allow that. Cancer is the work of the devil because cancer brings death and death is the enemy of God (1 Corinthians 15:26). Finally, death shall be swallowed up in victory. (1 Cor 15:54) Jesus conquered death and therefore conquered cancer.

The thief (Satan) cometh not but for to steal, kill and to destroy but I am that they might have life and that they might have it more abundantly.
John 10:10

Every good gift and every perfect gift is from above, and comes down from the Father of lights, with whom is no variableness, neither shadow of turning.
James 1:17

God is the author of life and every good gift but the devil is the author of all kinds of sickness and disease.

What about Job?

He was a righteous man and committed no sin. We see a conversation in heaven between God and Satan where the devil (who is an accuser) challenges Job's devotion to God. Satan argued that Job only worshipped God because God protected and blessed him. Satan declared that if he put sickness upon Job then Job would curse God and forsake Him. We can see from this passage that Satan not God is the author of sickness. This was a great trial of faith on the part of Job for even his wife told him to curse God and die but Job did not.

At the end God restored everything to Job in double measure. Why double? Because of his trial of faith. So just because you are sick you cannot say "I'm being tested by God" (James 1:13) - instead take authority over the devil and be healed in Jesus Name.

There is a great difference between your faith being tested or stretched from that of God putting sickness on you to test you. In Exodus 15:26 the bible says, "**I am the Lord who healeth thee**" Putting sickness on someone and allowing Satan rule over you are two entirely different things.

Be strong in the Lord

When we break God's laws as they did in the Old Testament the devil had room to attack them but when they obeyed God the devil had no opportunity. Jesus fulfilled the law for us and so sickness should not be allowed in our bodies. Of course sickness and disease are not always the result of sin and can be just an attack of the devil (as in the case of Job).

> **Finally, my brethren, be strong in the Lord, and in the power of His might. Put on the whole armour of God, that ye may be able to stand against the wiles of the devil.**
>
> Ephesians 6:10, 11

We are in a spiritual battle and sometimes there are casualties but thank God He has given us weapons to fight with and armour to protect us (Ephesians 6:10-18).

Chapter 20
Healing in the Bible

Isaiah 53:4-5—Jesus fulfilled this prophecy when he destroyed the power of sickness and disease upon the cross. This scripture is mentioned again in **Matthew 8:17** how Jesus took our infirmities and bare our sicknesses. Again, in **1 Peter 2:24** it is written how by the stripes of Jesus we are healed. Throughout Matthew, Mark, Luke and John we see the healing ministry of Jesus. For example, in **Matthew 4:23, 25** it says Jesus healed all manner of sickness and disease. In **Matthew 8:1** a leper asked Jesus if it was His will to heal and Jesus said yes, and the leper was instantly healed.

Here are some other references you can look up:

Matthew 9:2-8, 9:18-30. In Matthew 10:1 Jesus gave power to His disciples to cast out evil spirits and heal all manner of sickness and disease.

Matthew 12:10-22, 14:14, 14:35, 36, 15:22-31, 17:14-21, 20:30-34,

Mark 1:30-34, 1:39-42, 2:1-12, 3:1-15, 5:2-16, 2:22-43, 6:53-56, 7:25-37, 8:22-25, 8:17-29, 10:46-52

Luke 4:33-41, 5:12-26, 6:6-10, 6:17-19, 7:2-10, 7:12-16, 8:27-56, 9:37-43, 13:10-16, 14:3-7, 17:11-19

John 4:46-54, 5:1-19, 6:2, 9:1-33, 11:1-44, 12:37-38

Acts 3:1-16 4:29-33, 5:12-16, 9:32-42, 14:8-11, 19:11-12

Jesus is the same yesterday, today and forever (Hebrews 13:8) and if He healed them in His day He still heals today. So let us put our faith in Jesus and believe and we shall see many healed by the power of God.

I would recommend that you read and meditate on all the healing references given so your faith will grow. The anointing upon your life will also increase as you feed on His Word and spend time with the Holy Spirit for it says in Zechariah 4:6 - *It's not by might, nor by power but by my Spirit says the Lord.*

For more healing testimonies, books and tapes visit our website www.ashkotecha.org